COLOR TEST

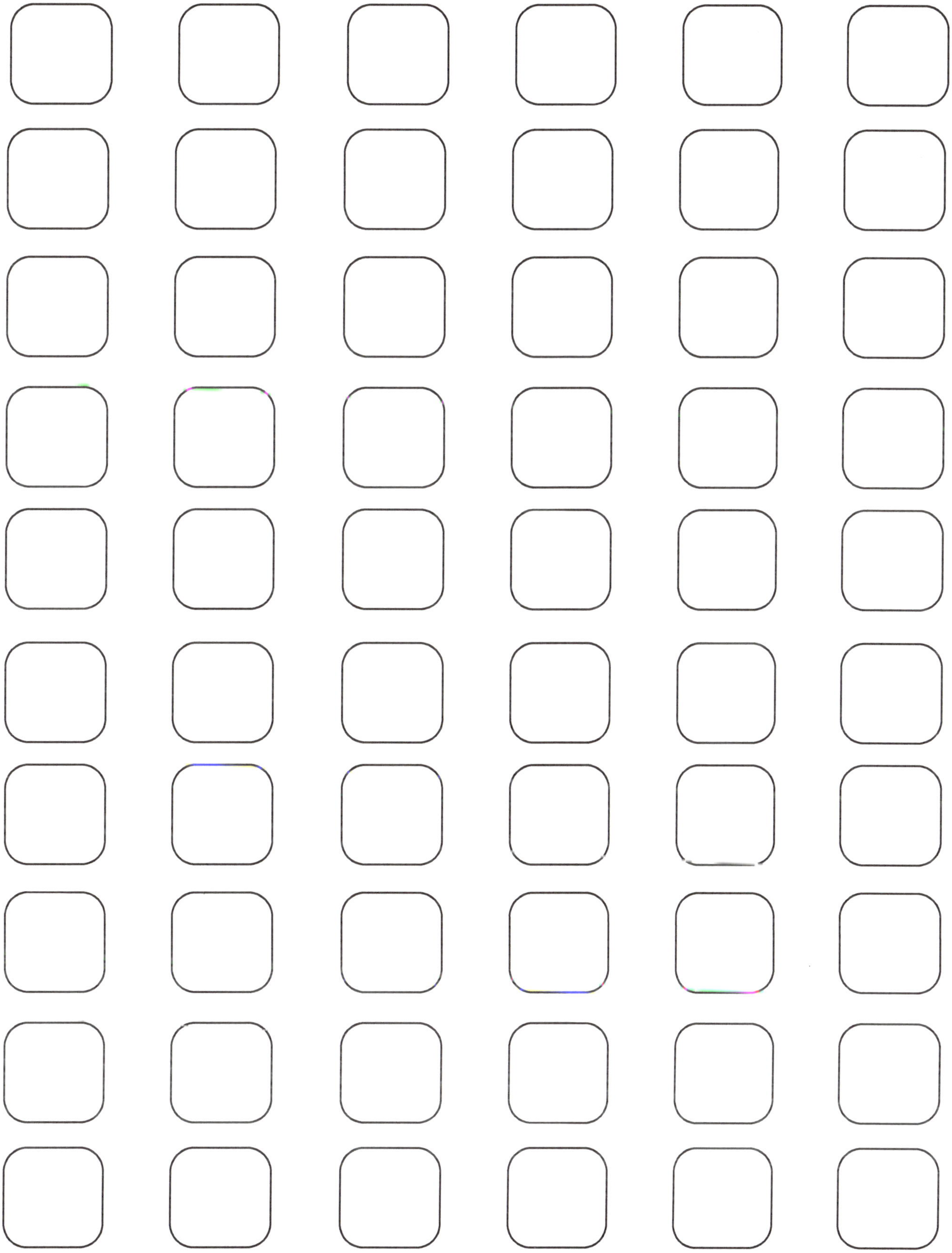

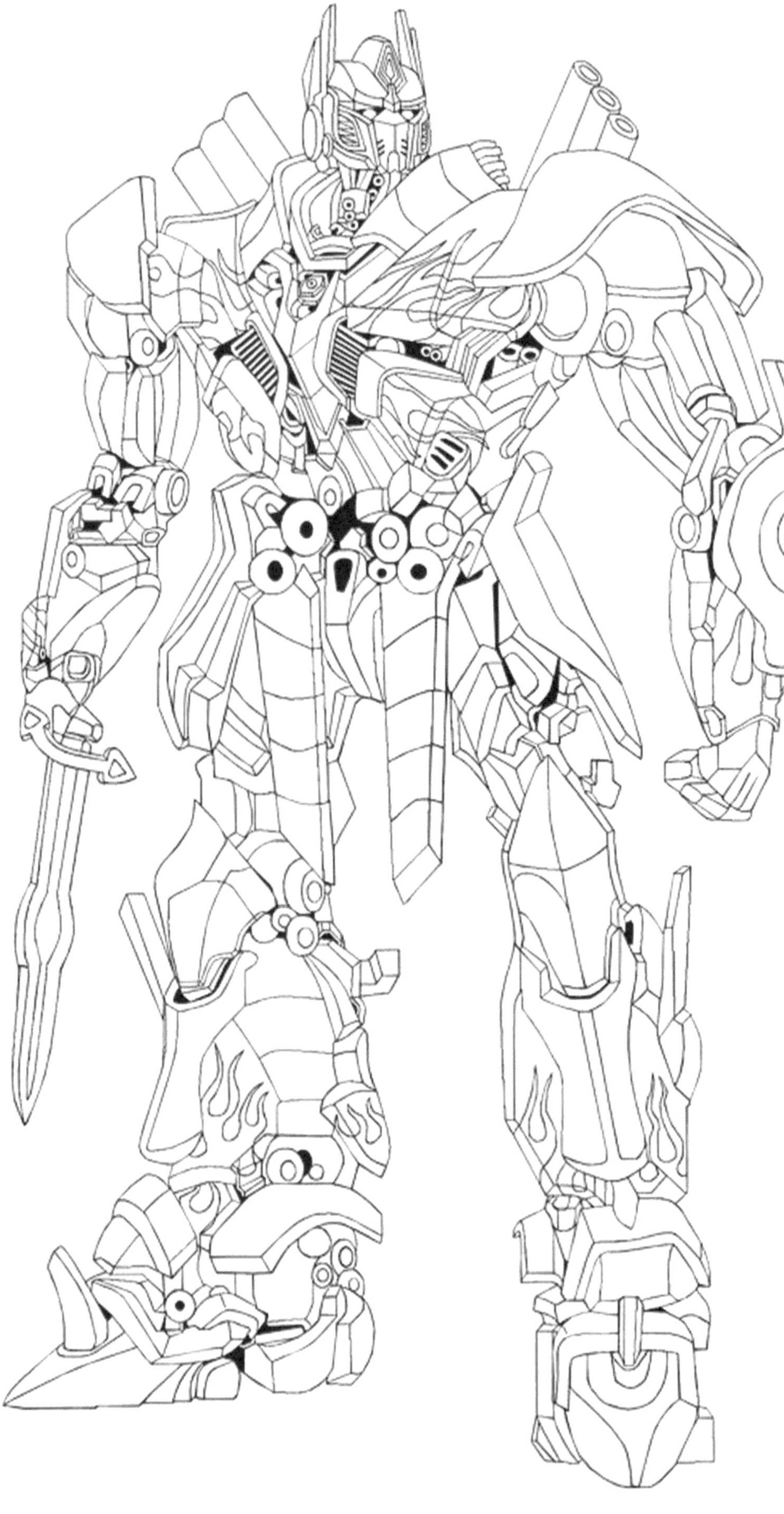

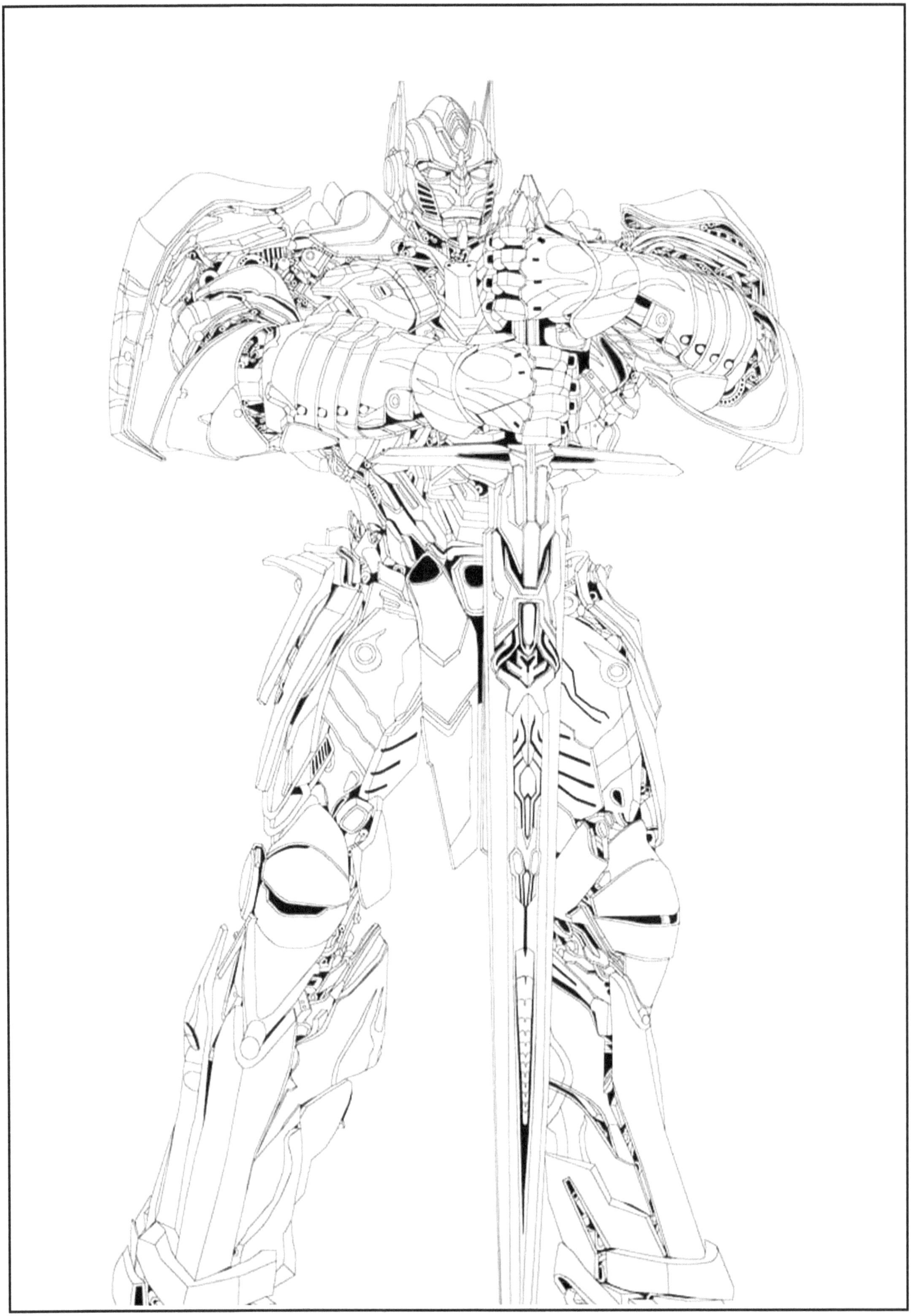

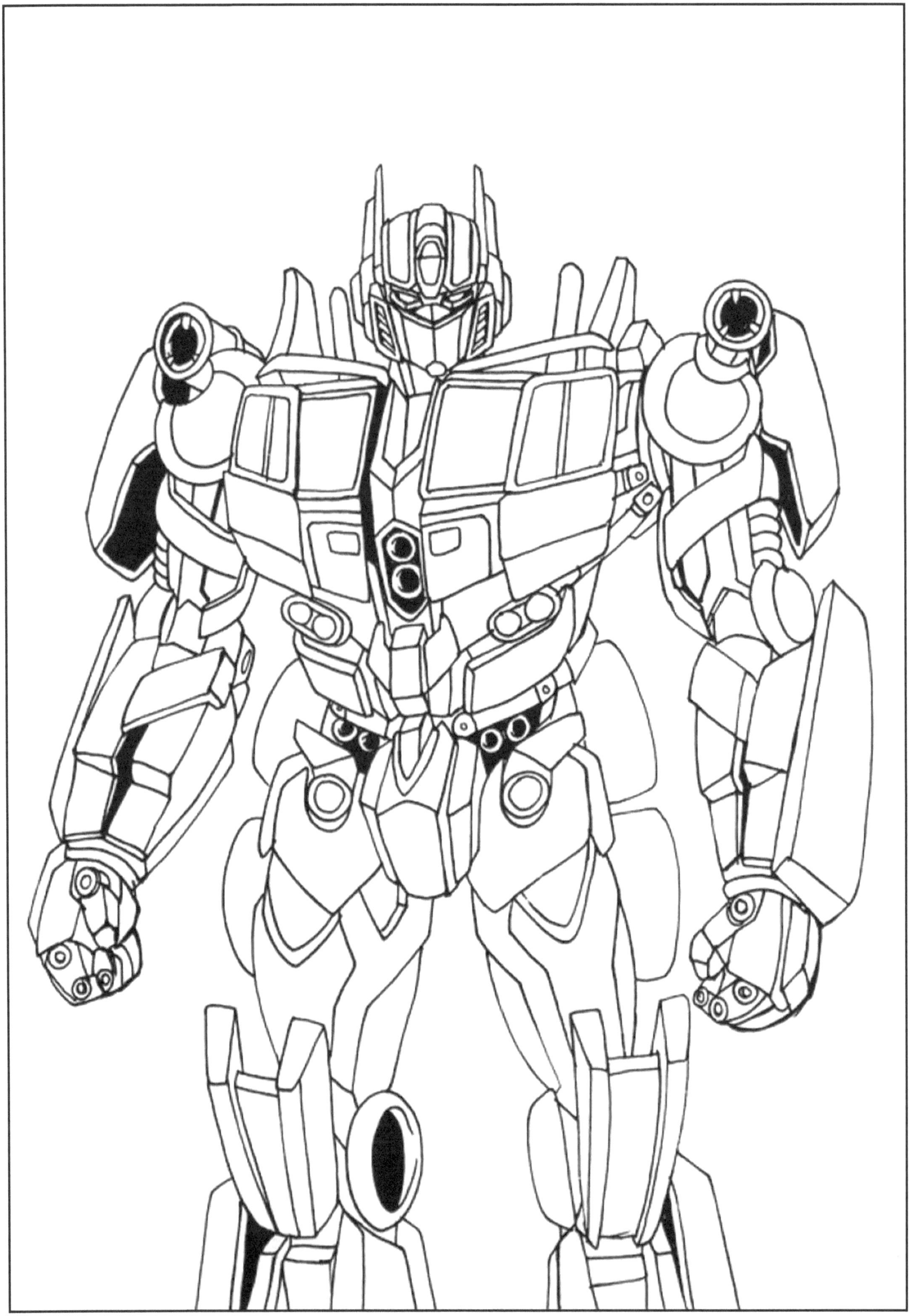

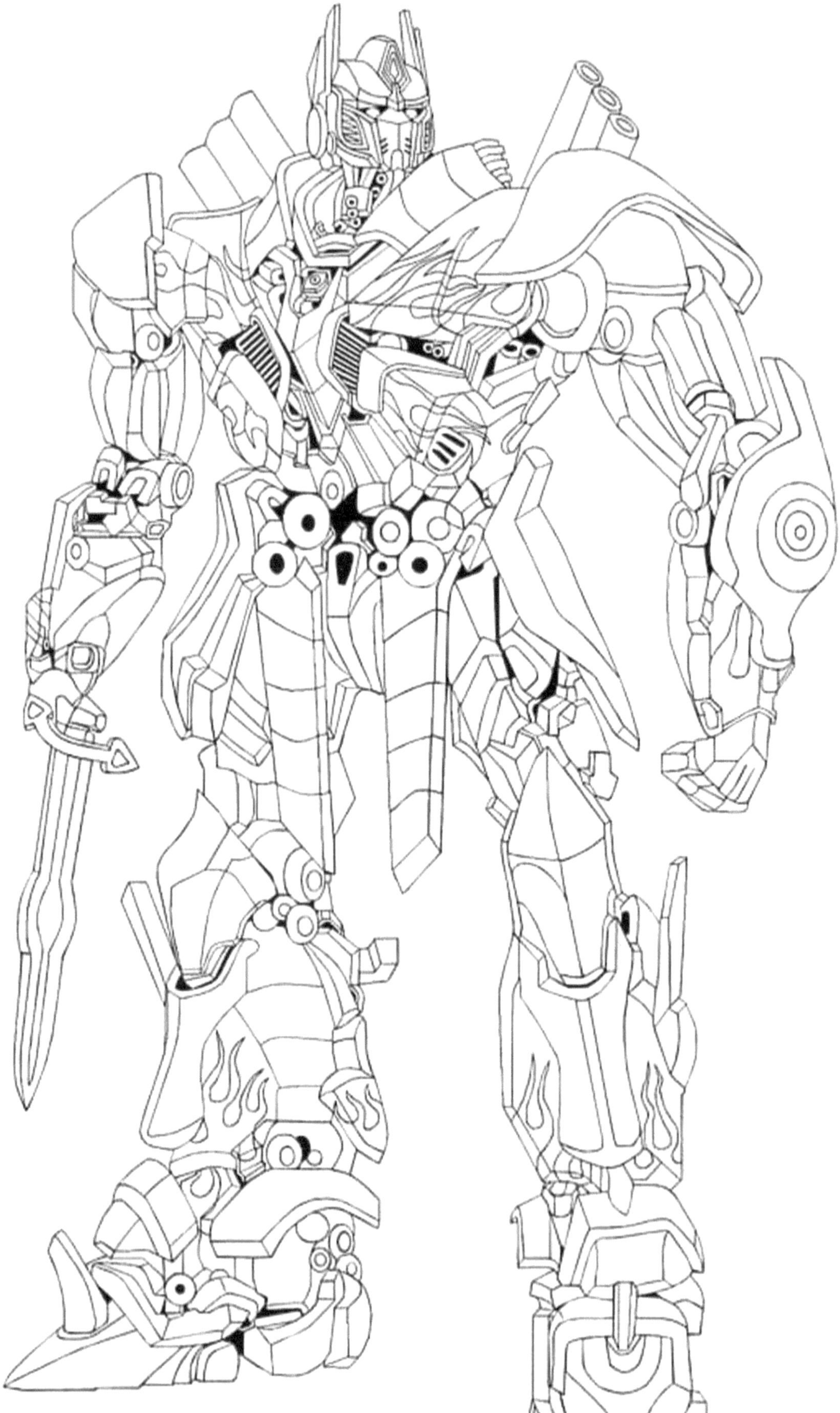

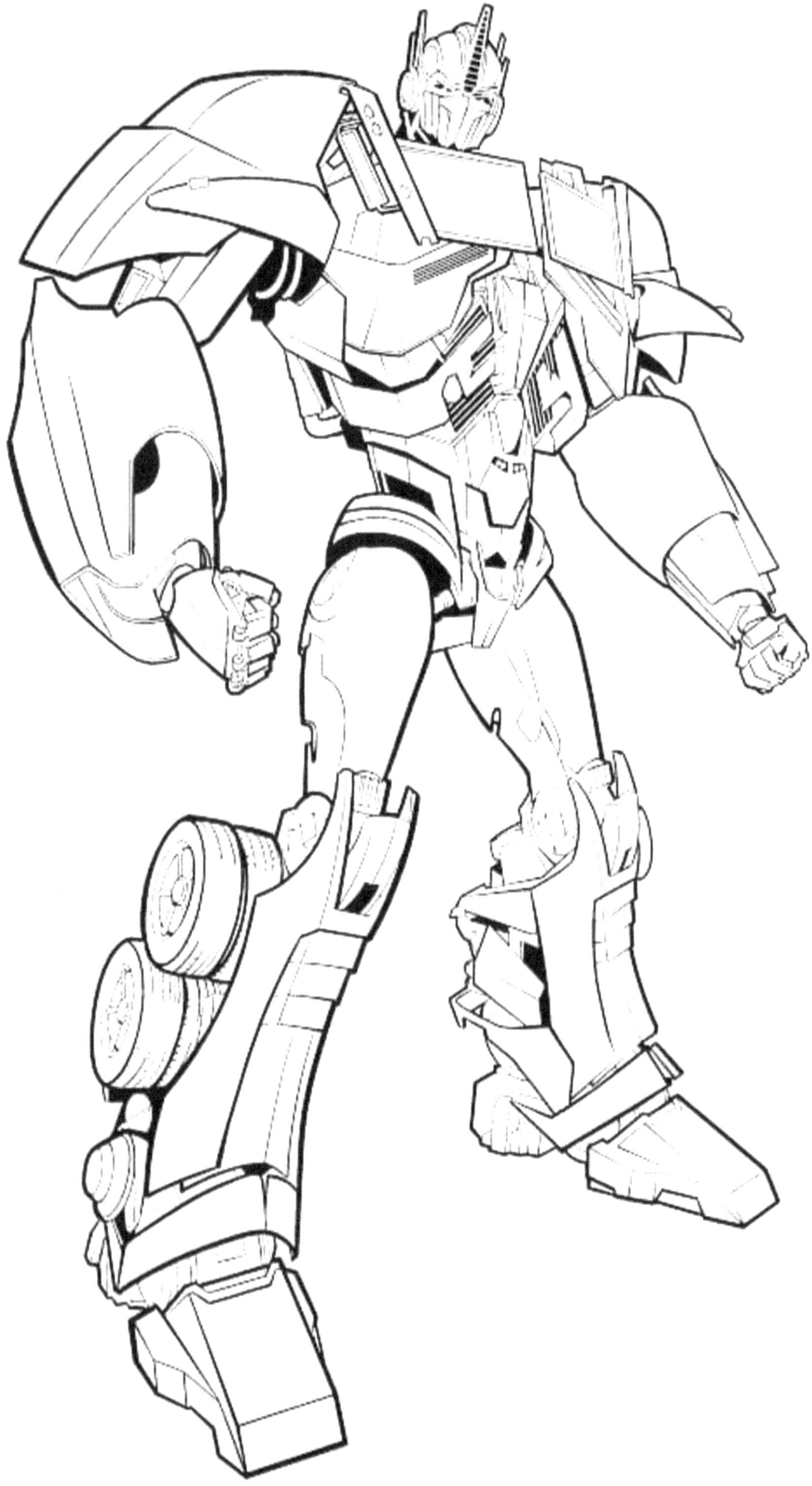

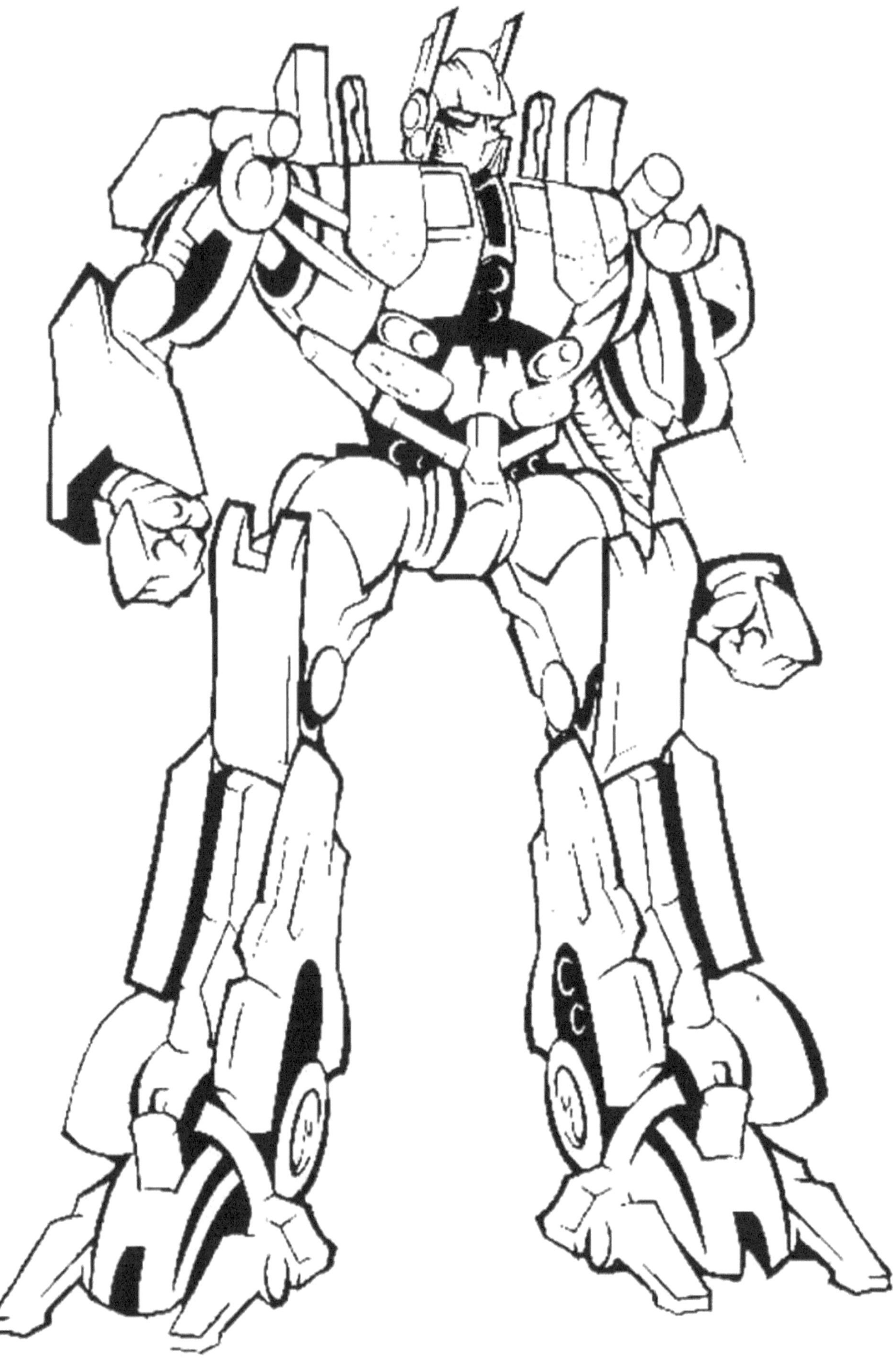

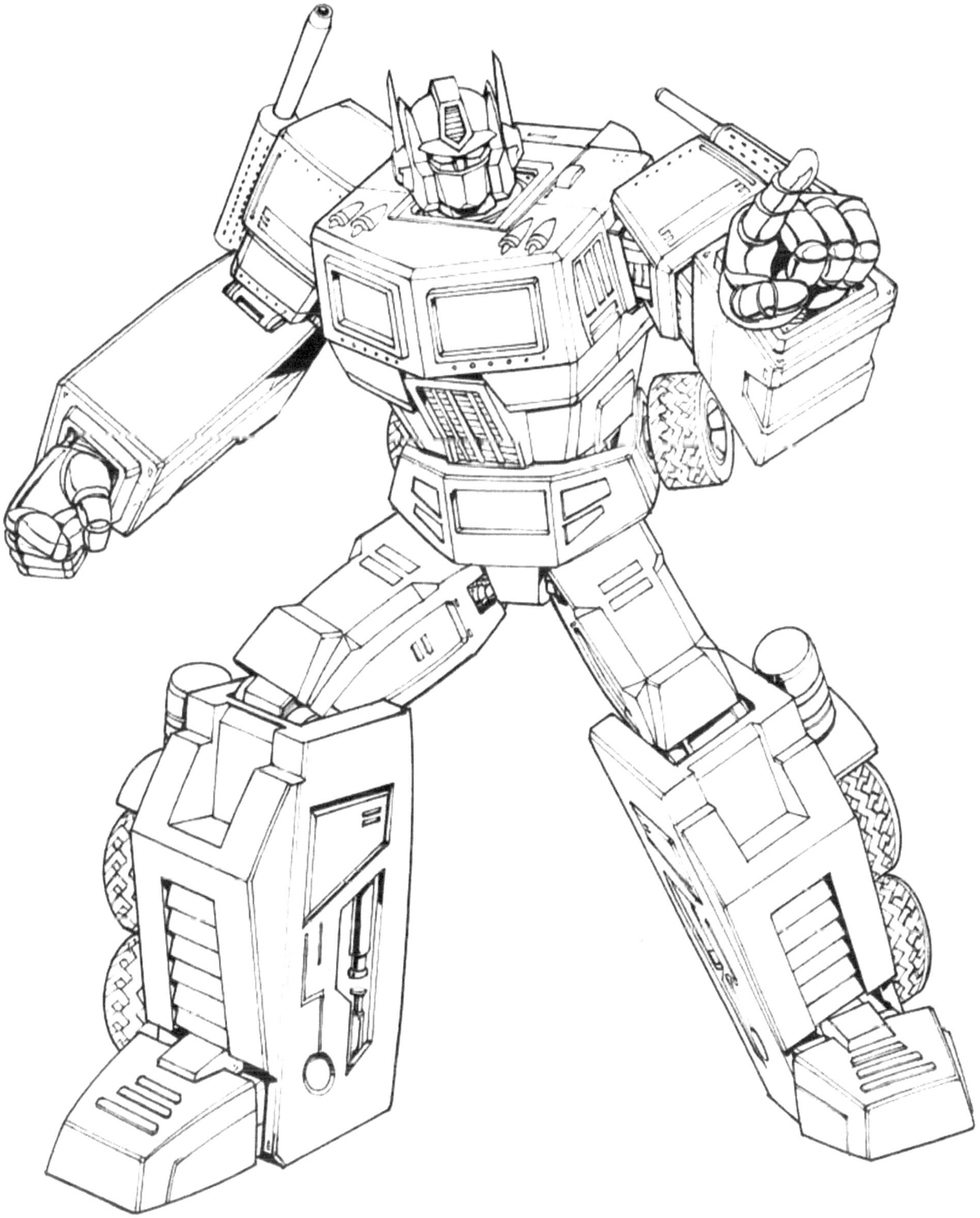

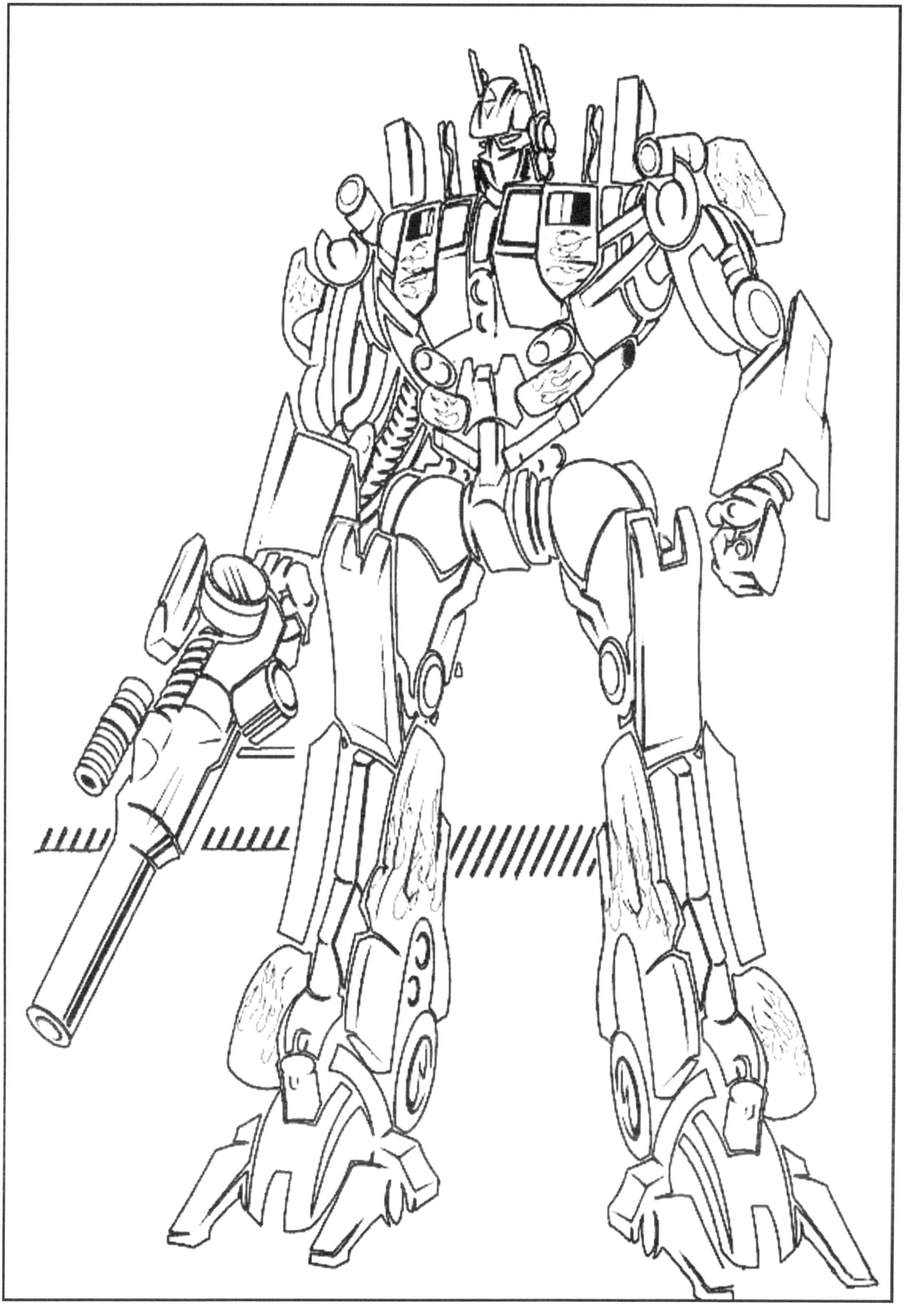

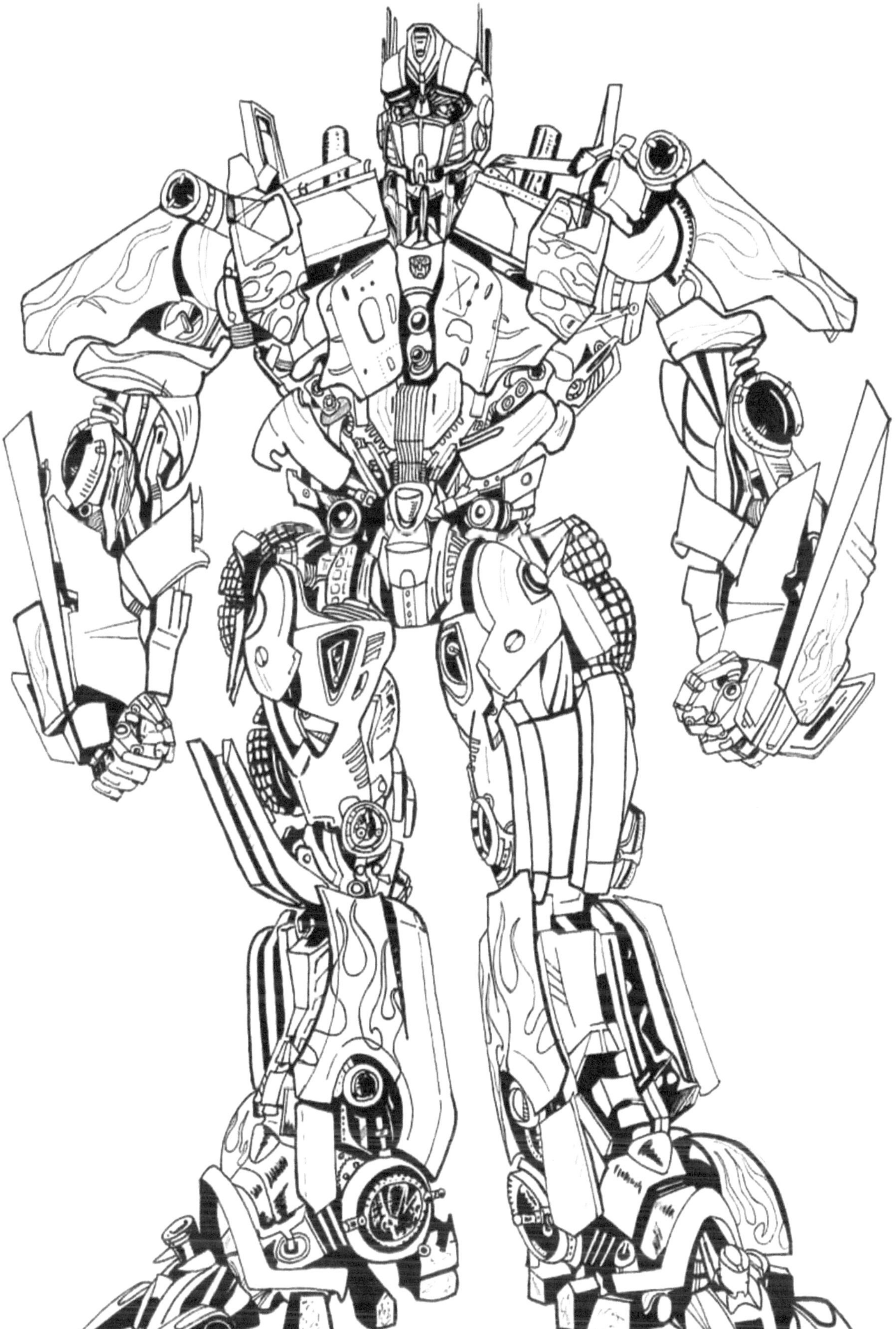

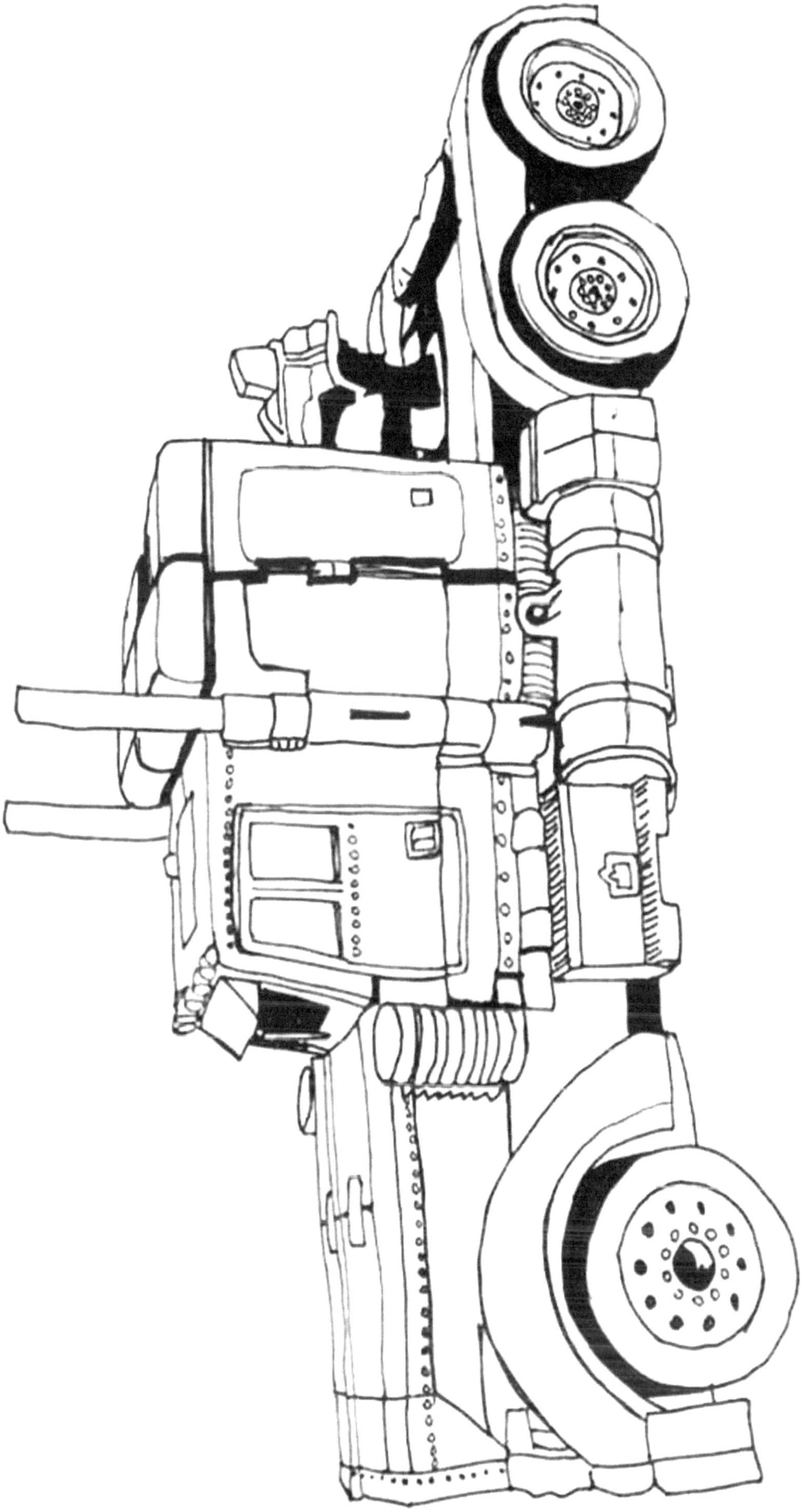

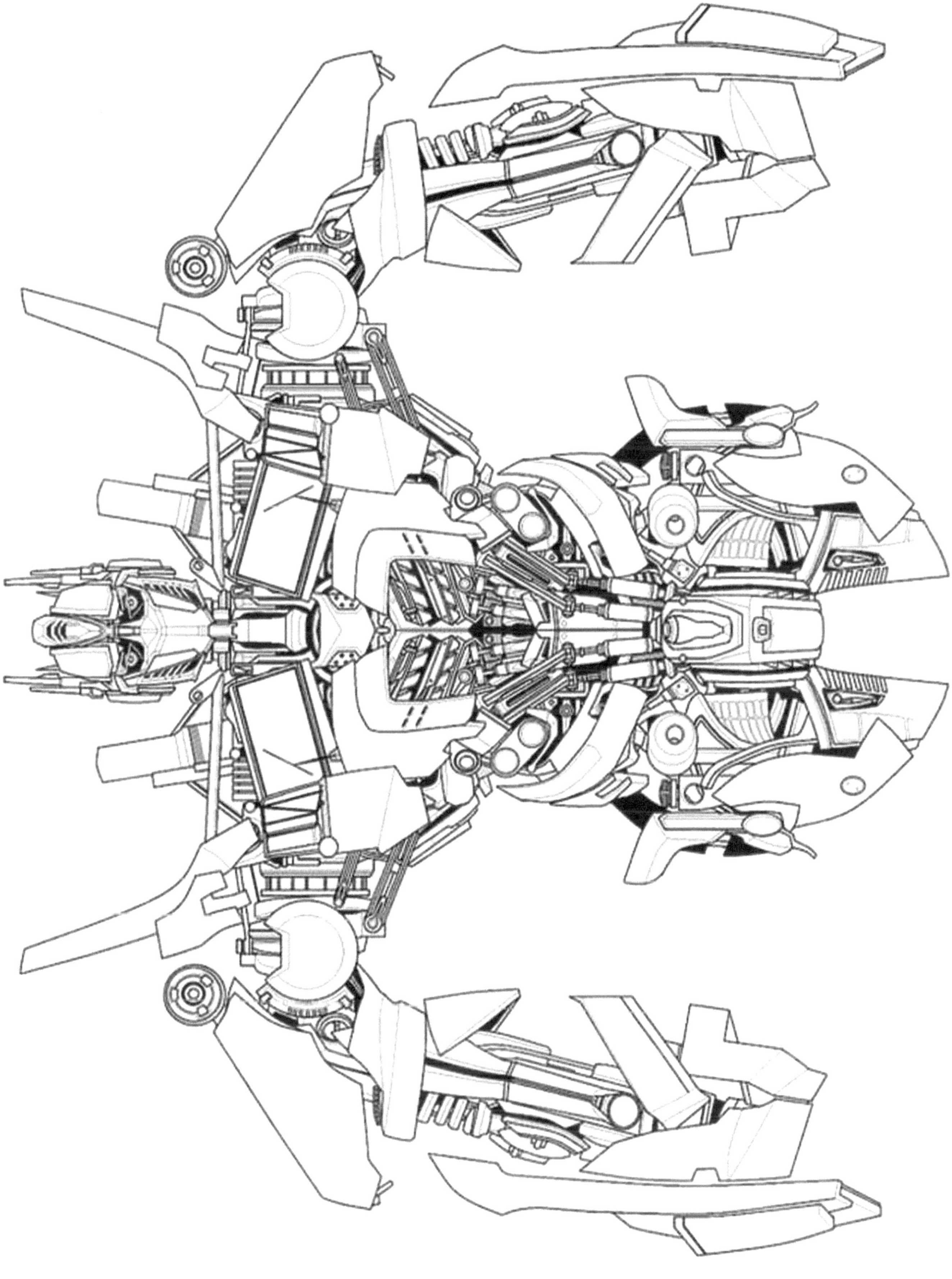

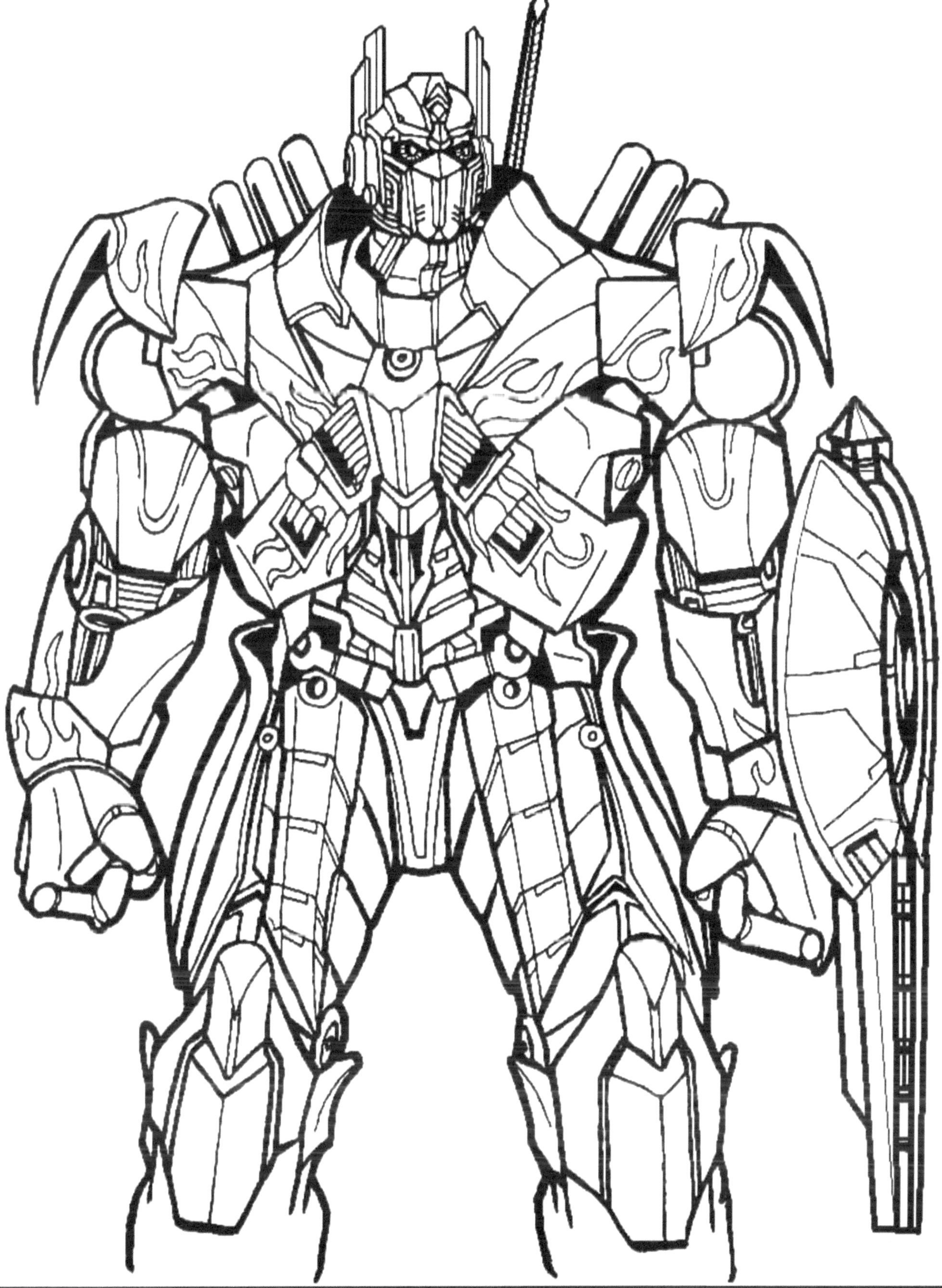

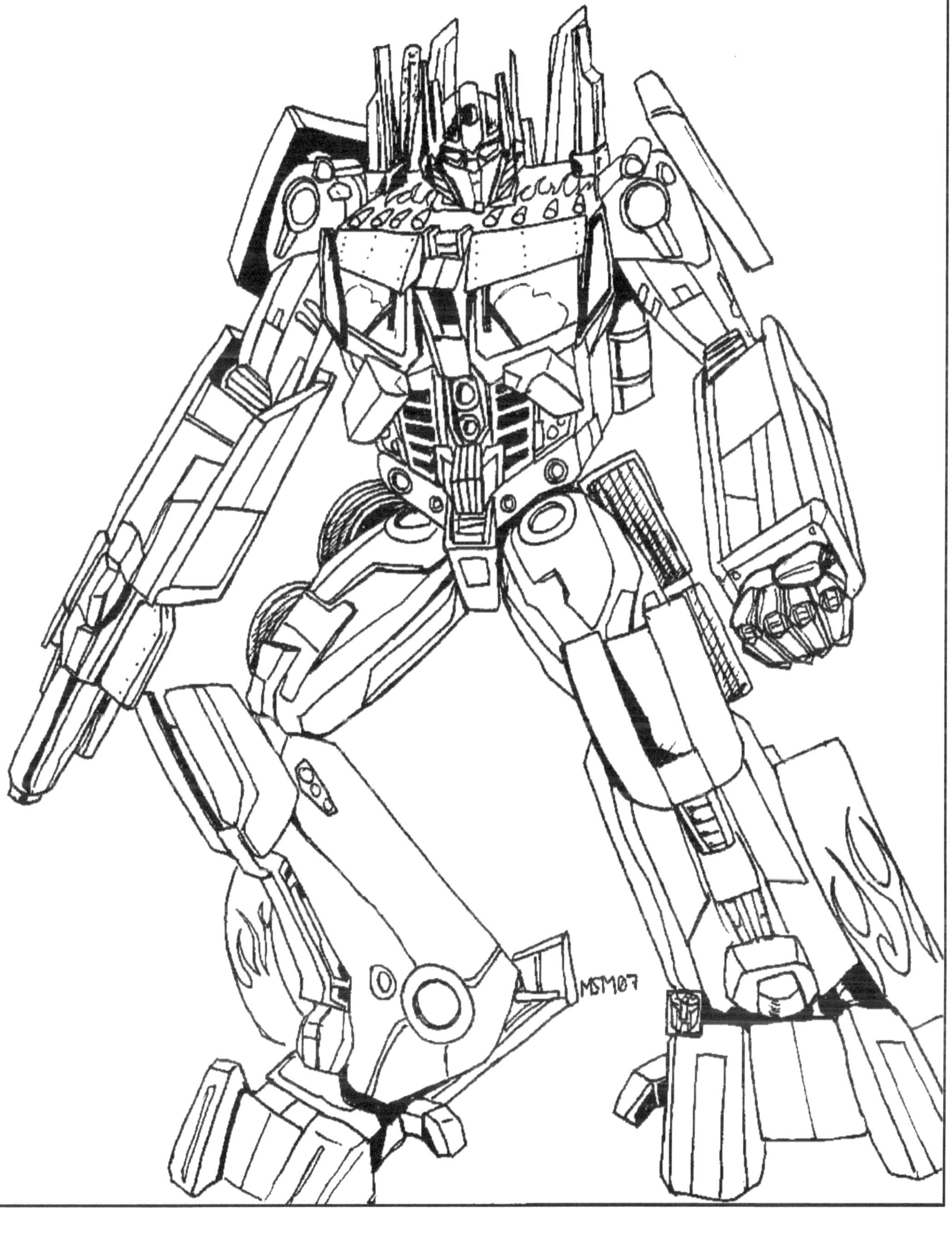
MSM07

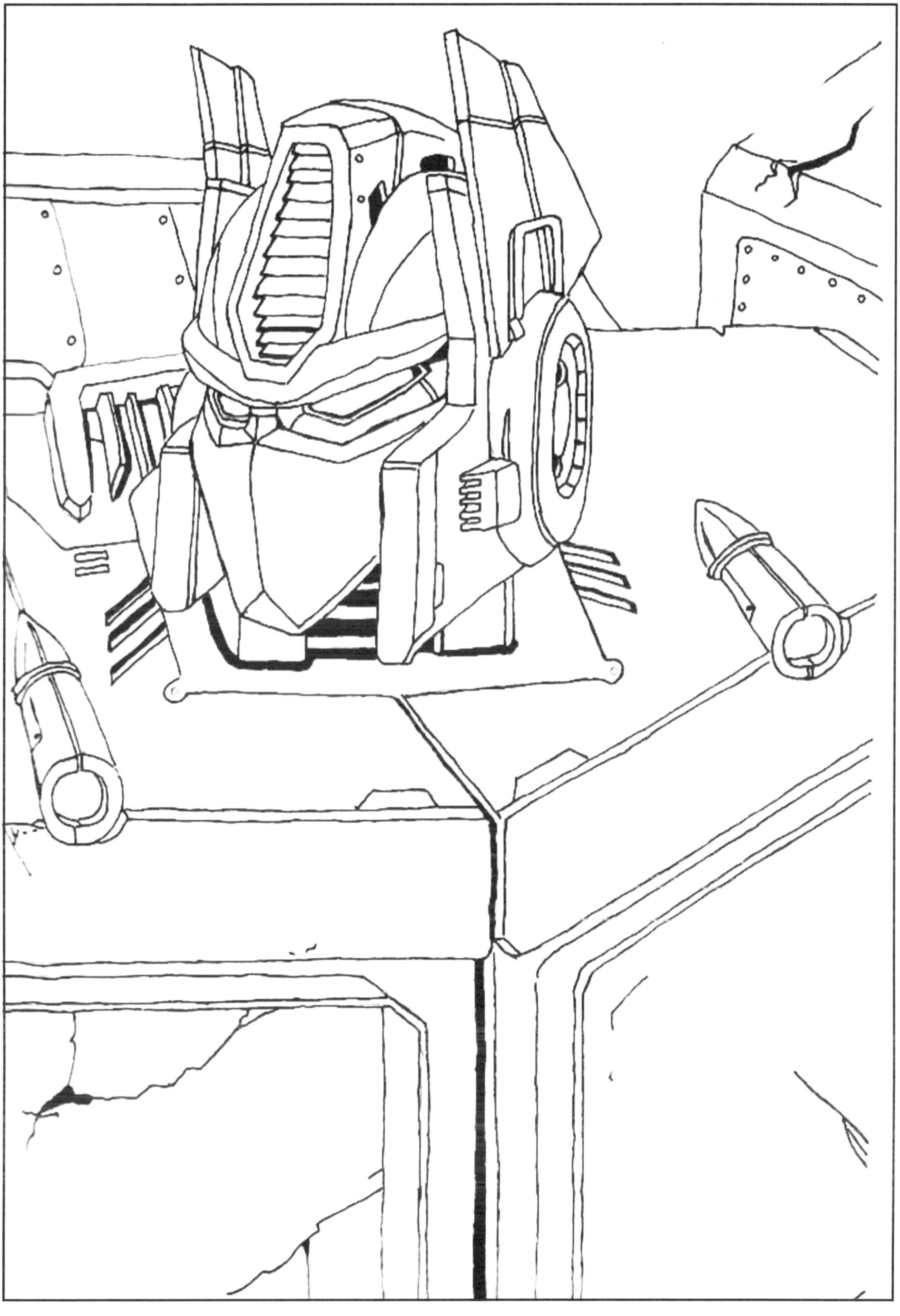

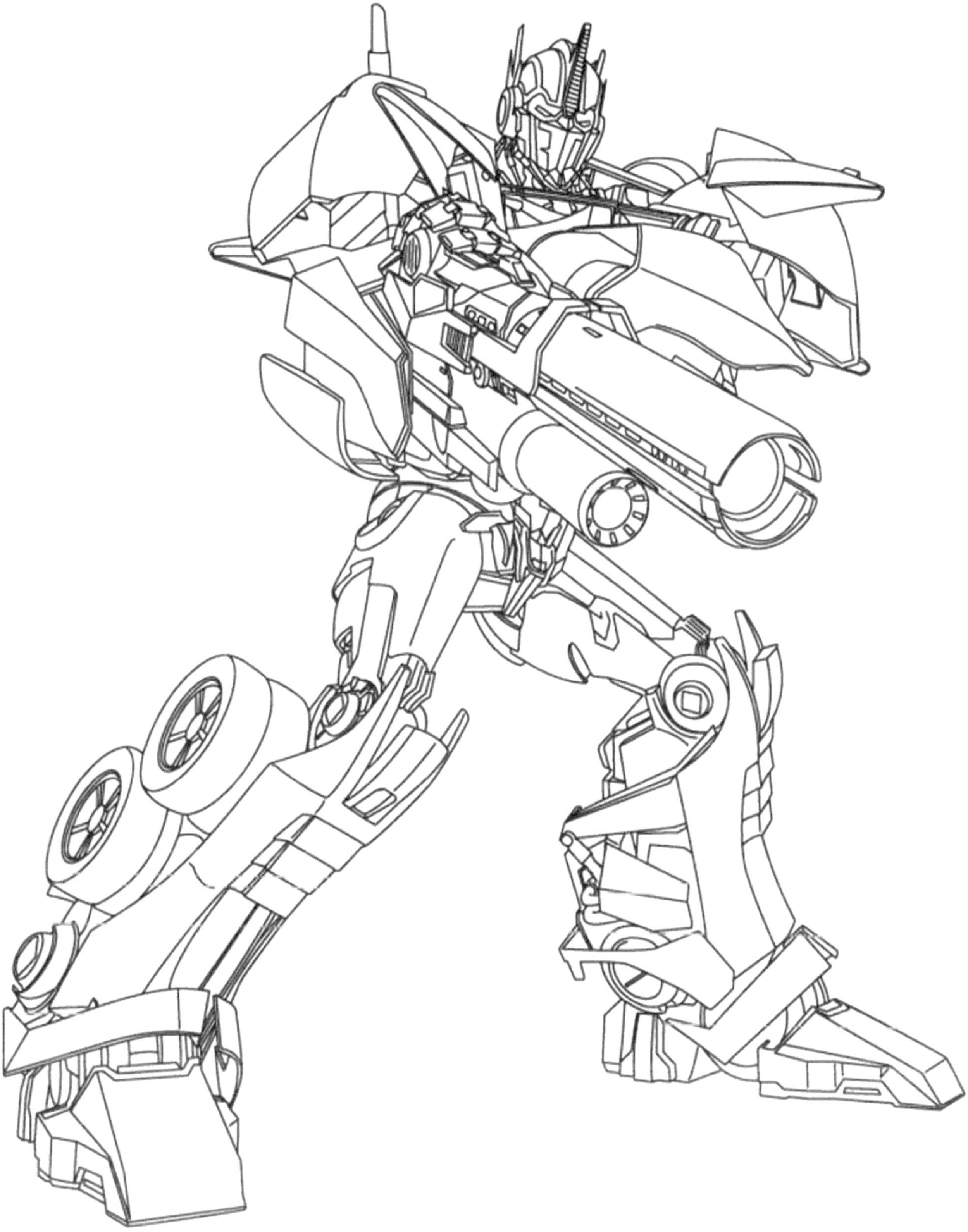

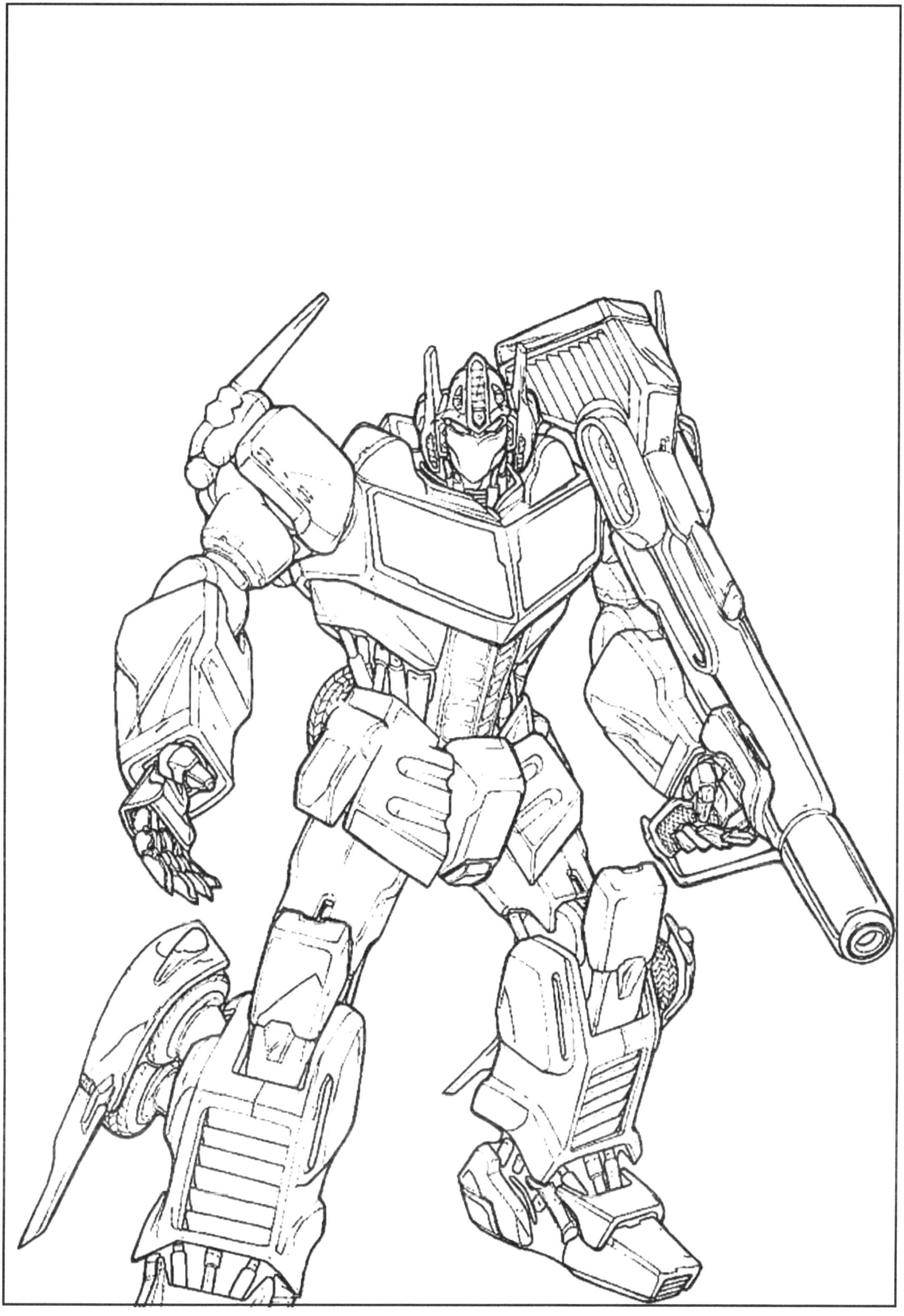

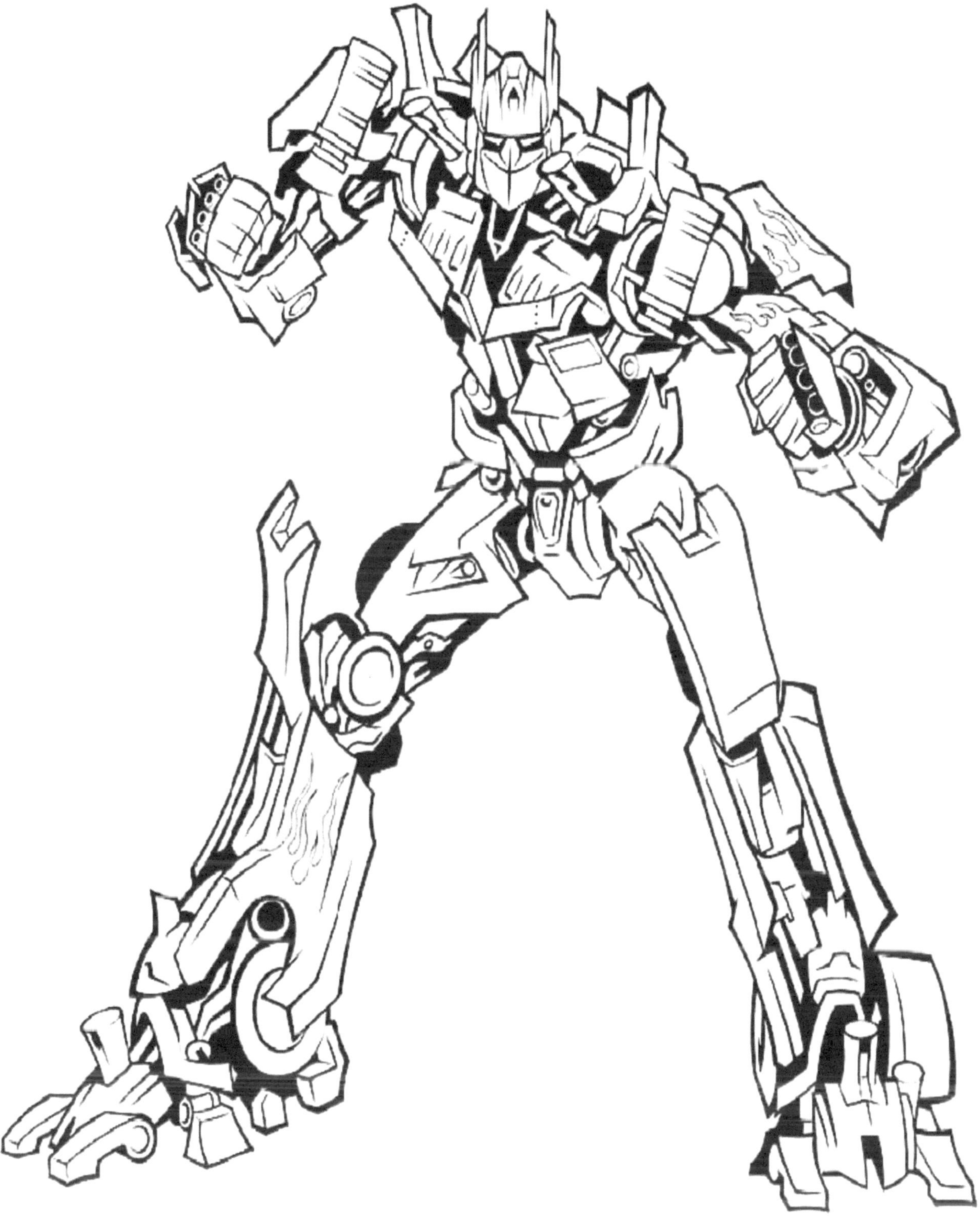

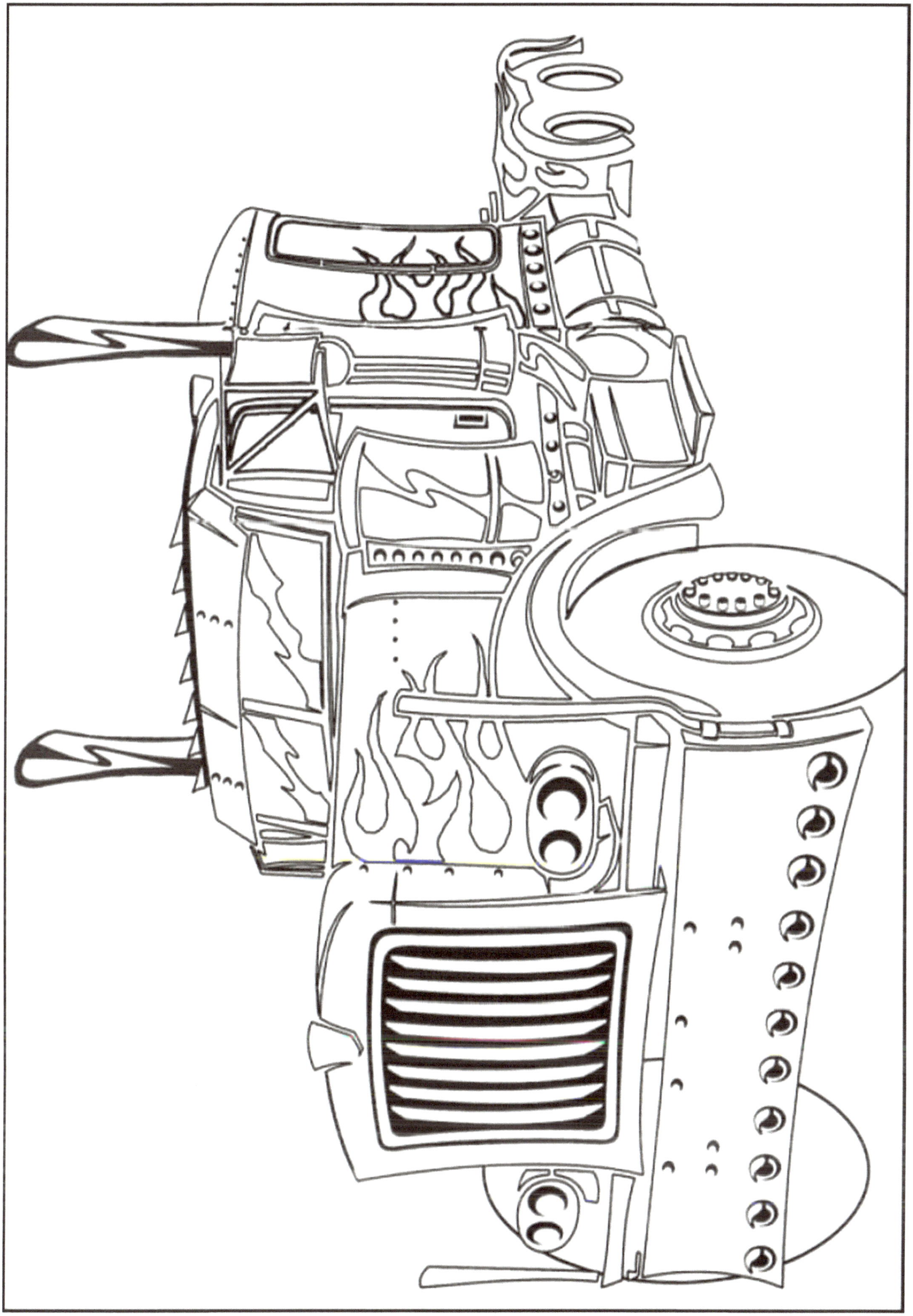

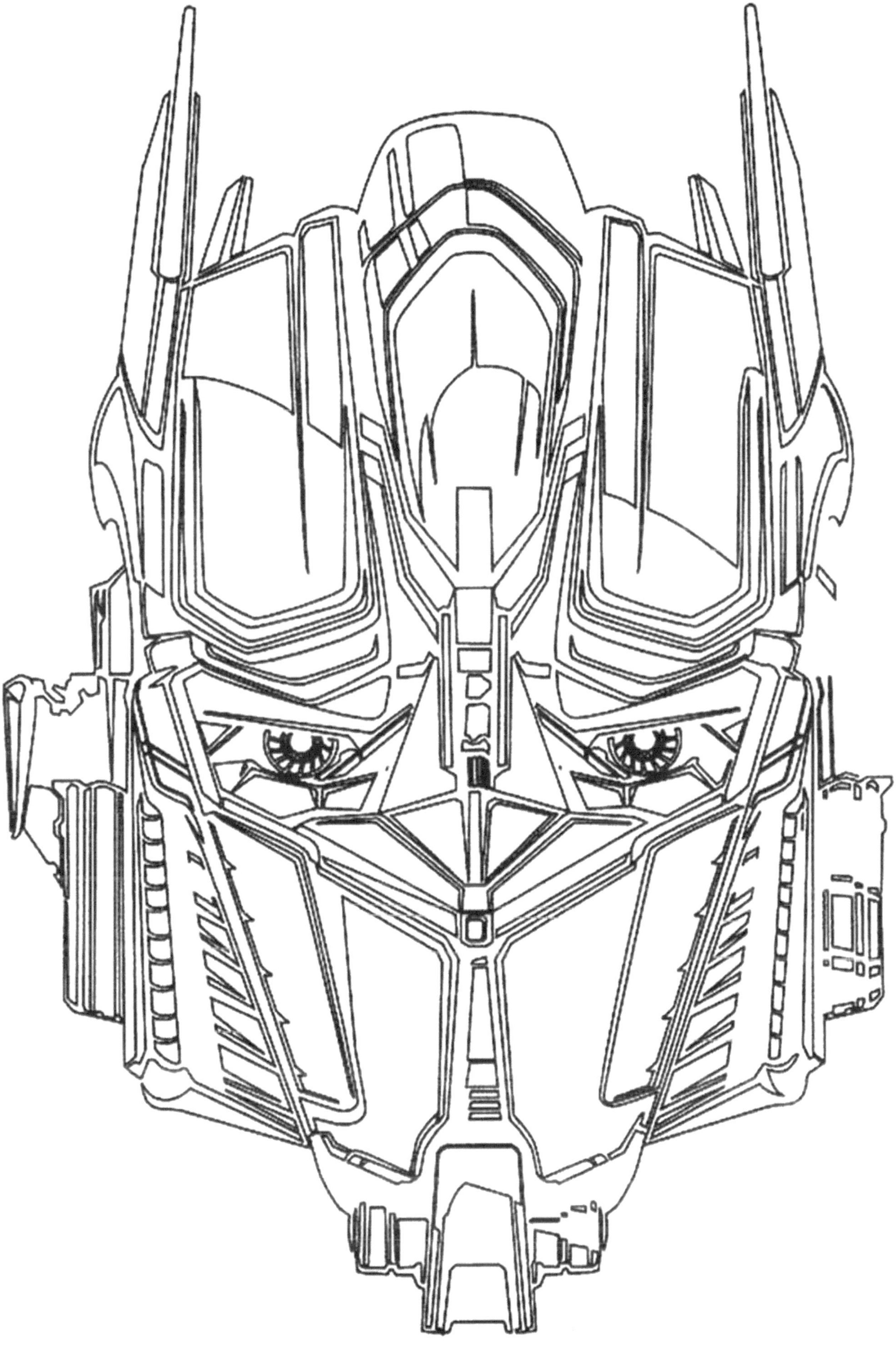

FAITH
A.F.T.

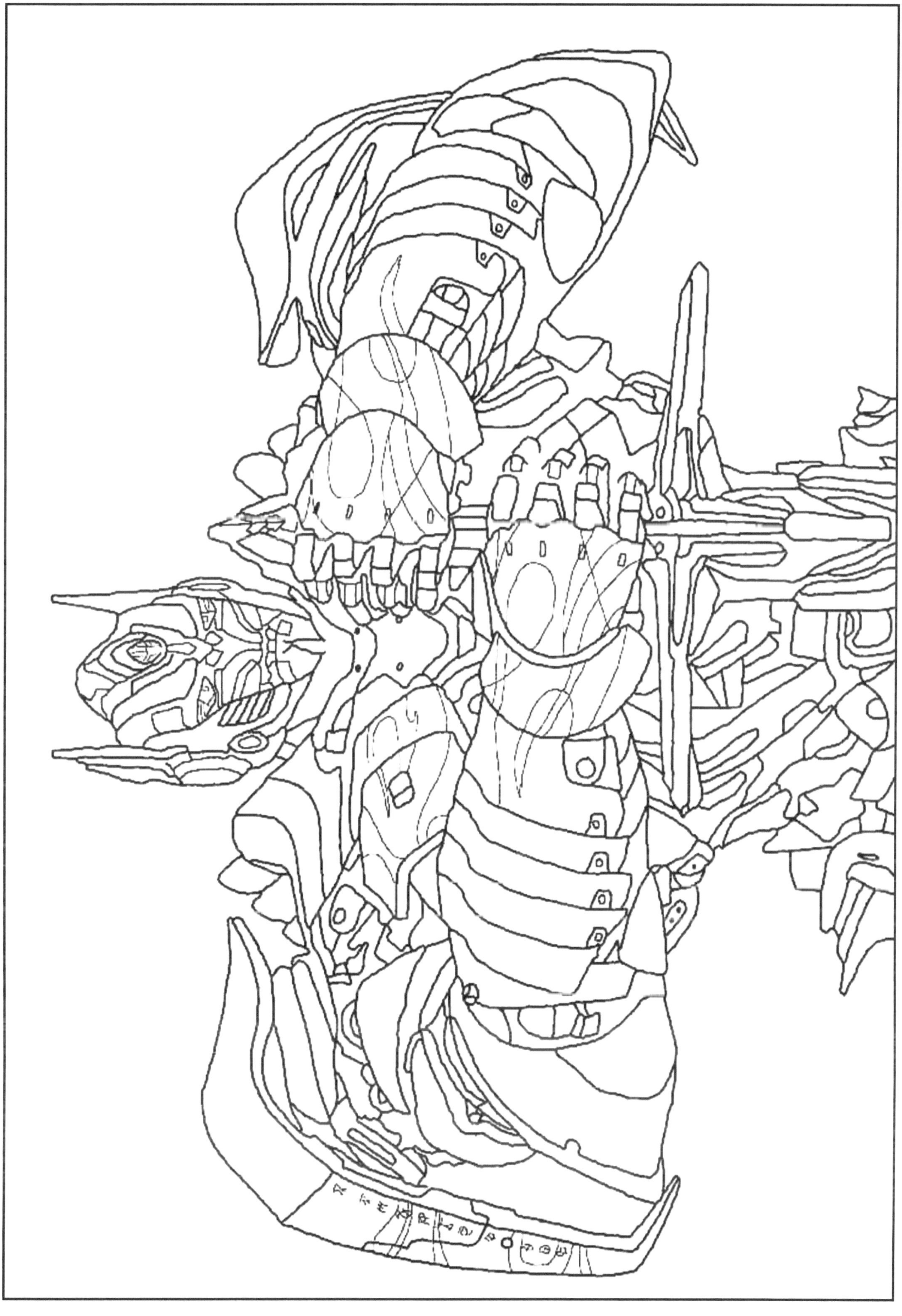

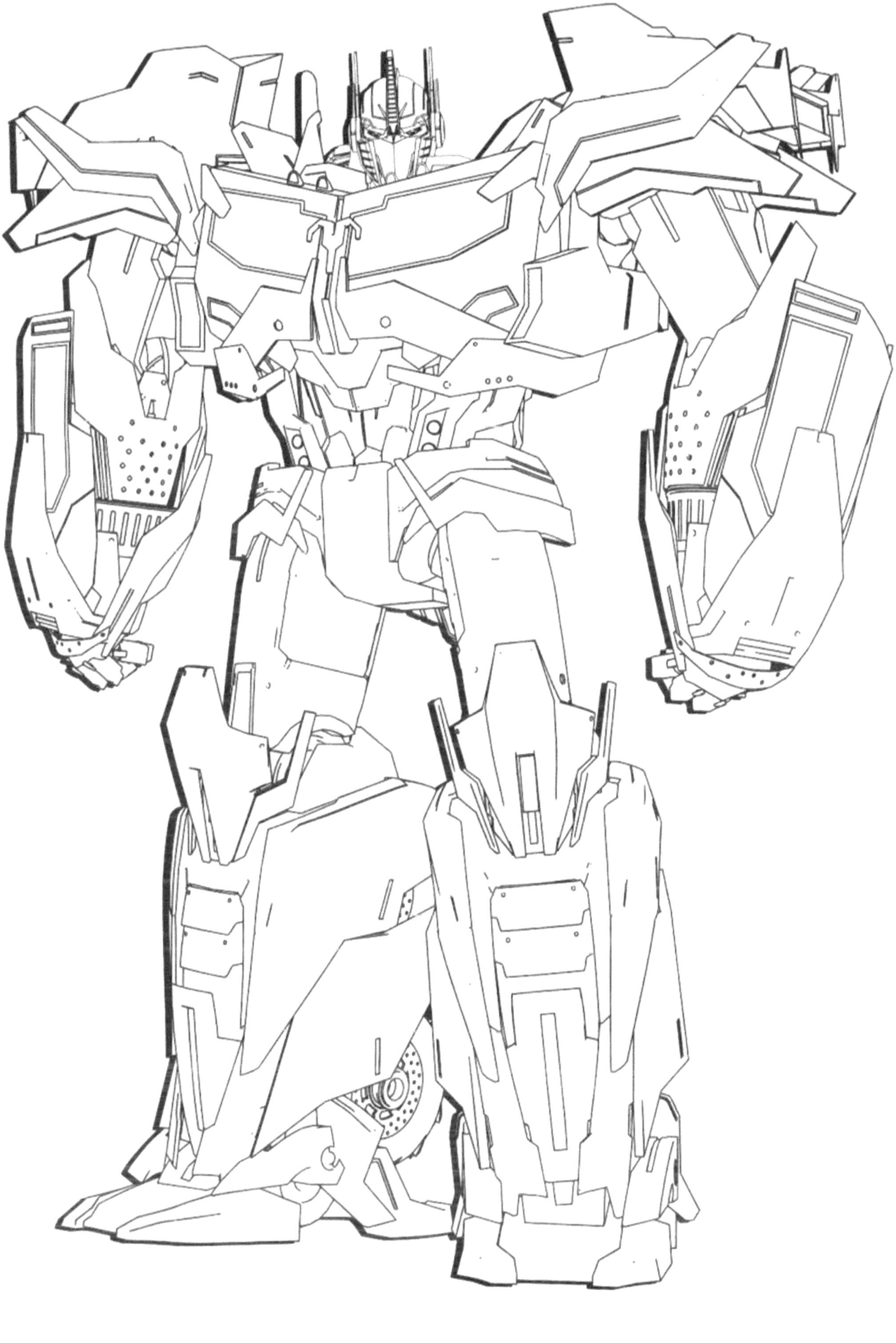

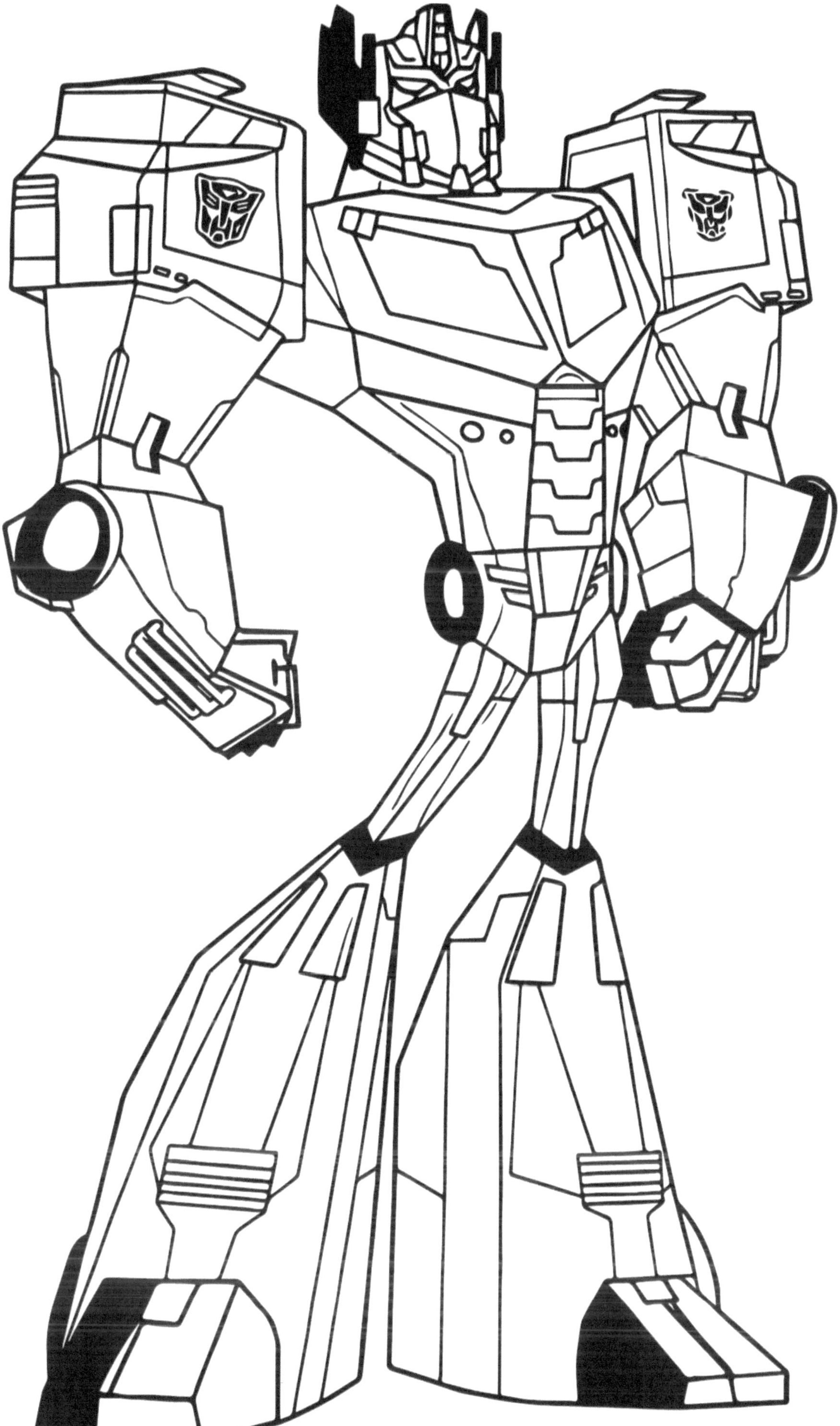

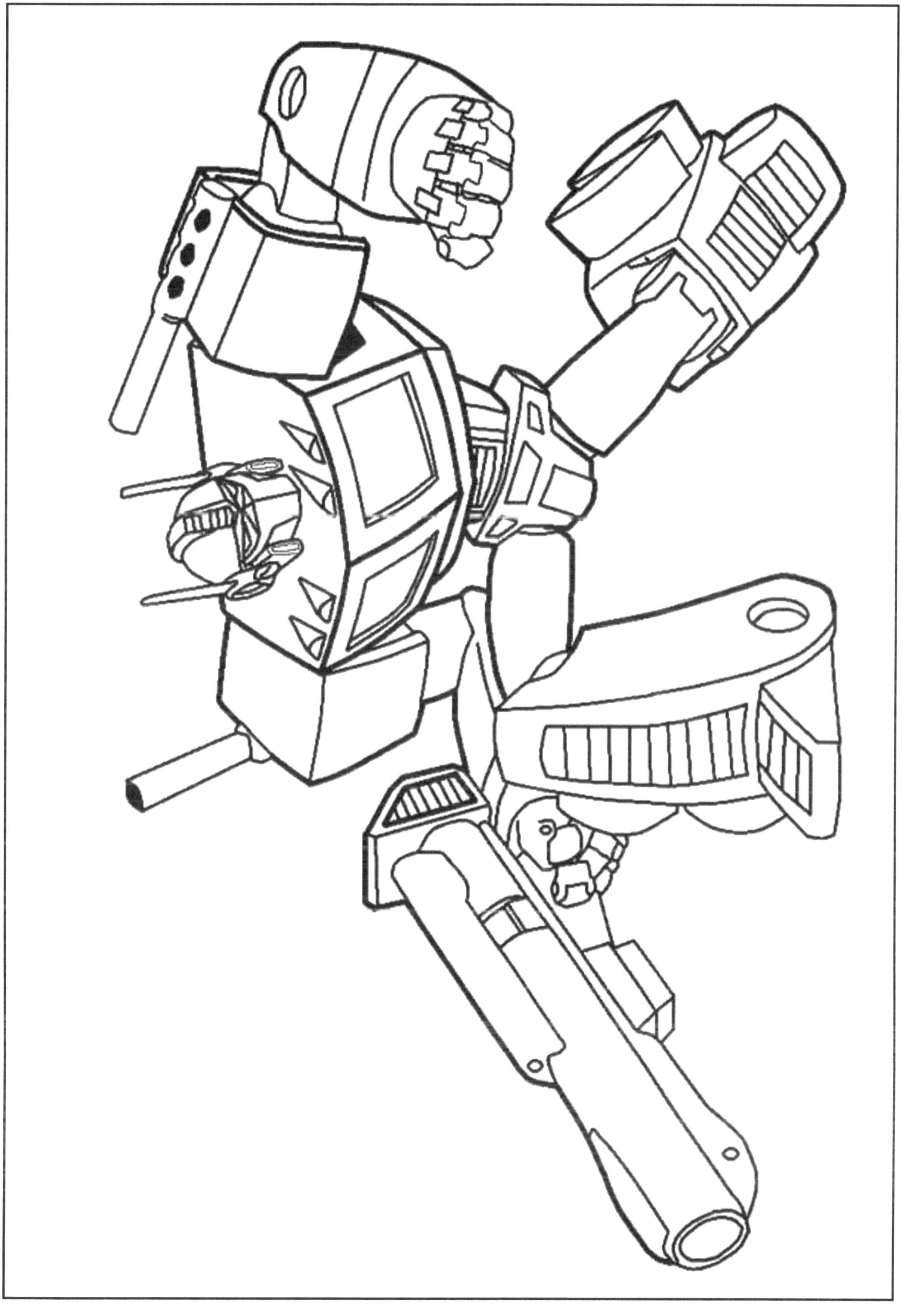

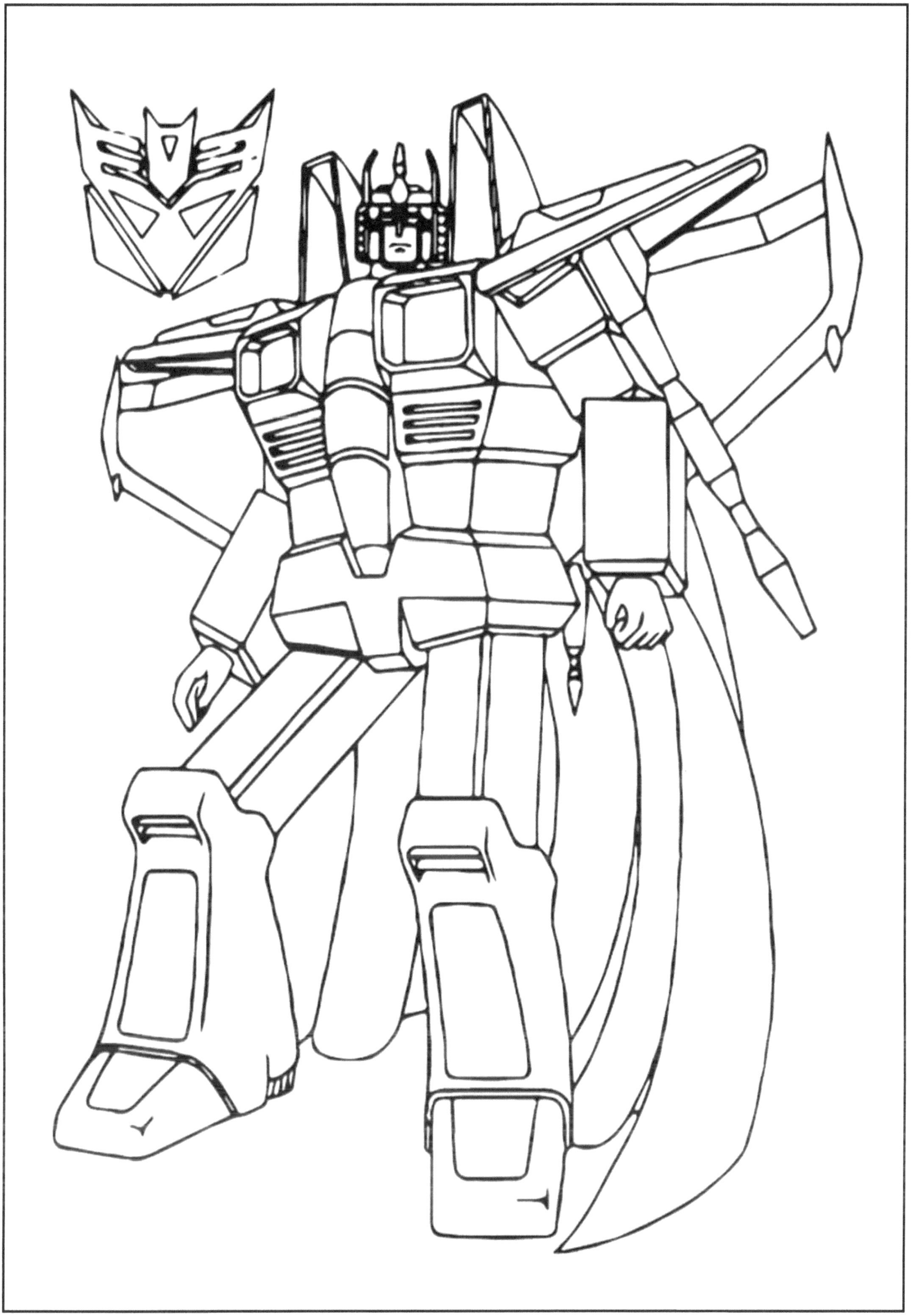

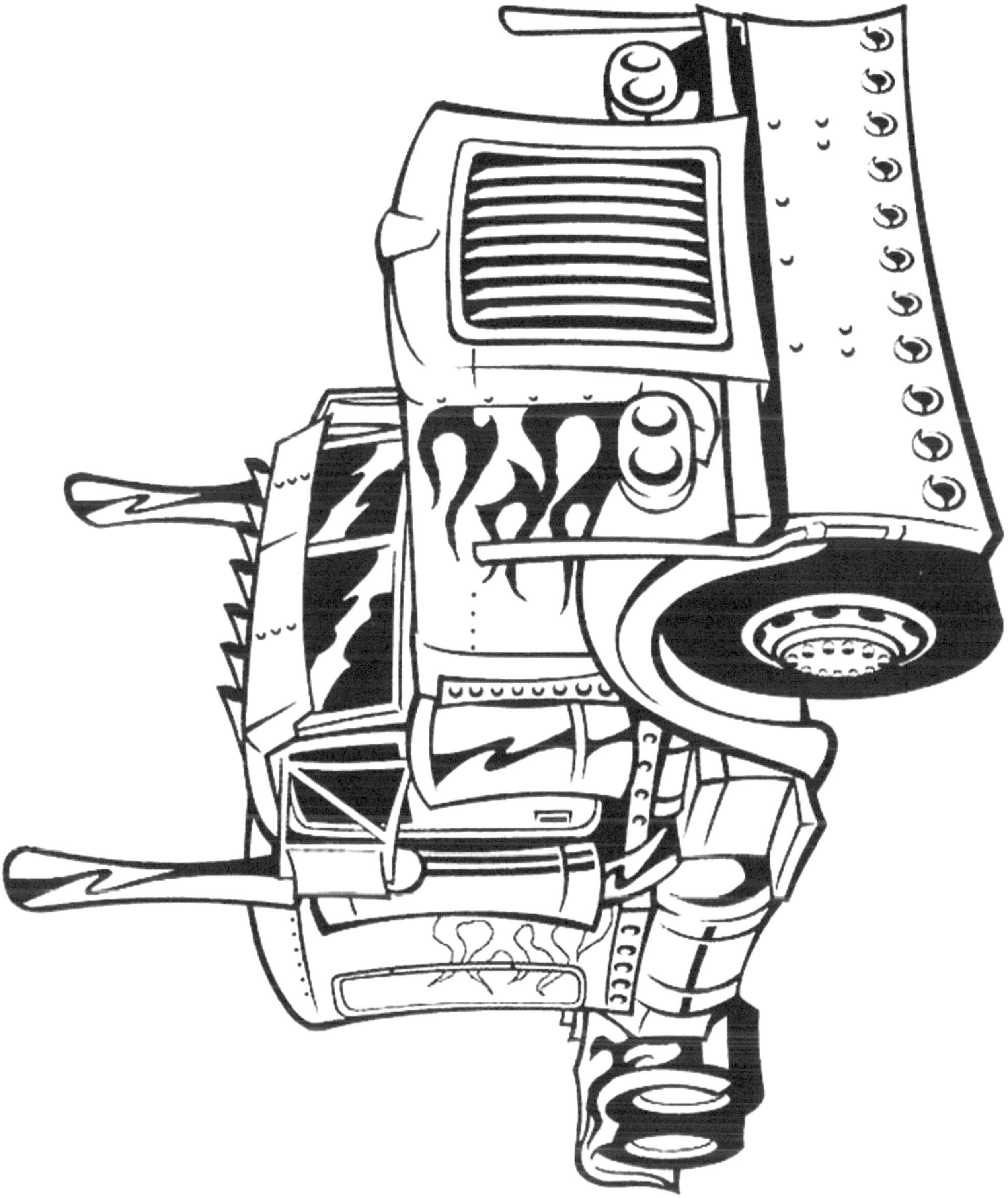

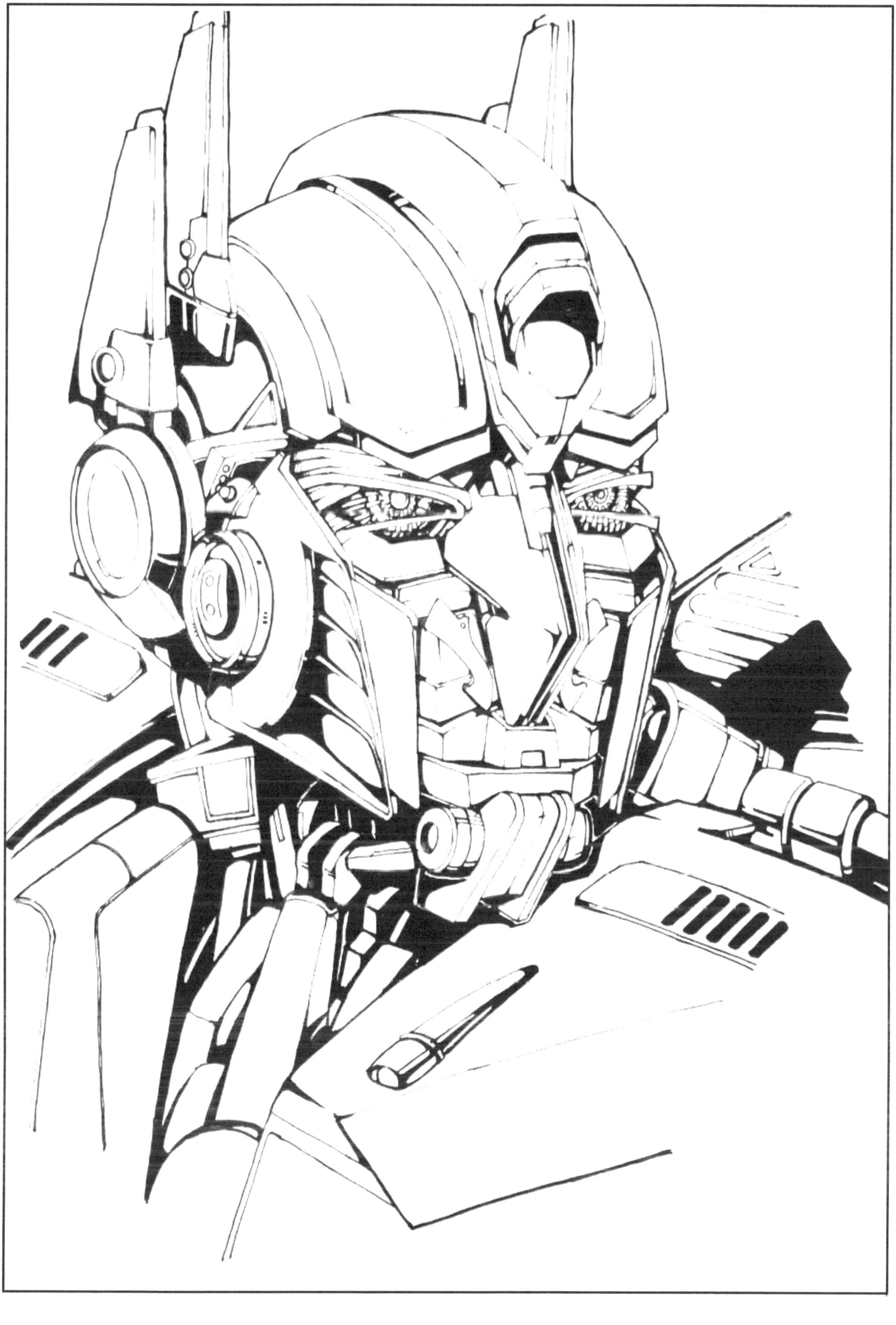

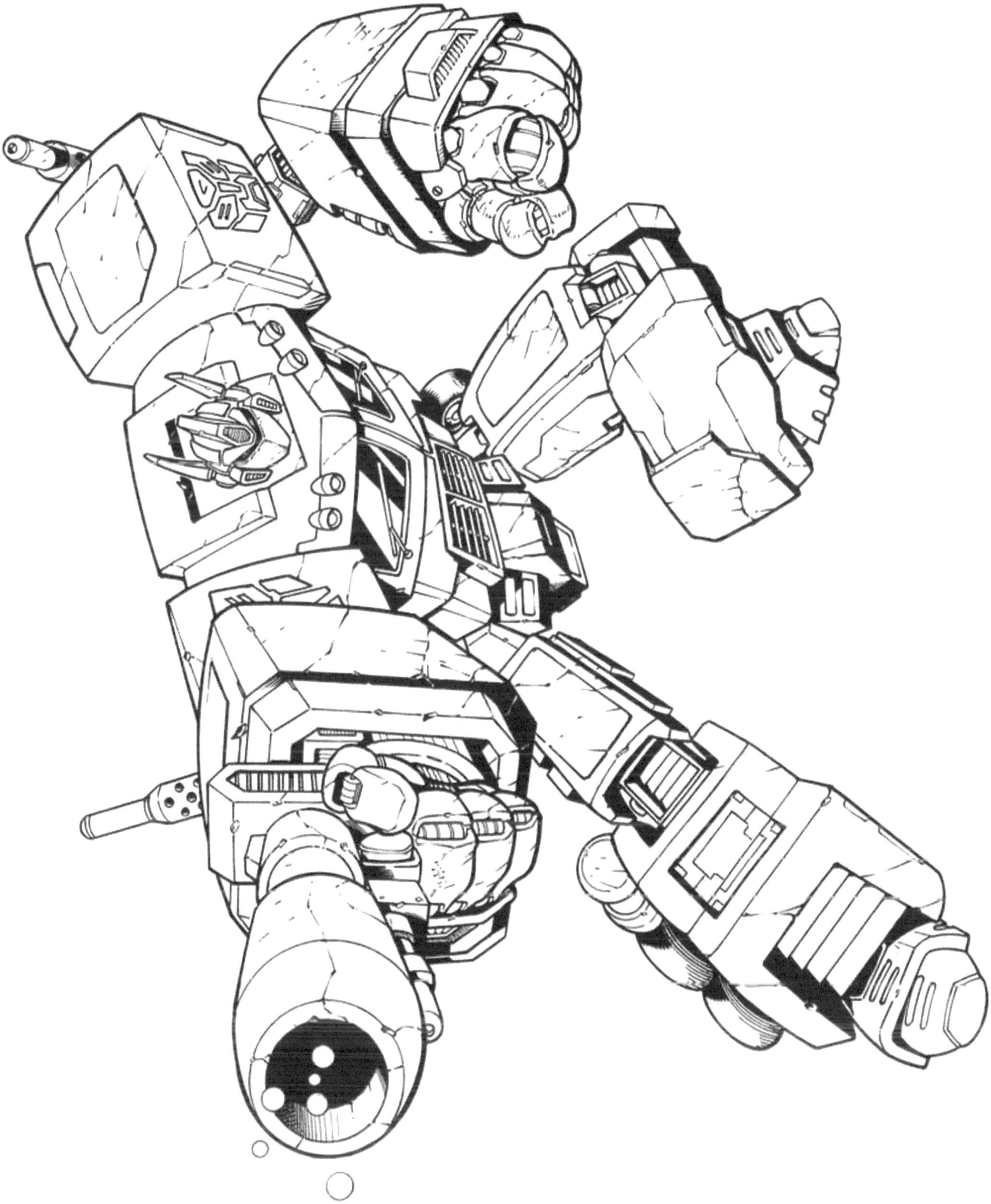

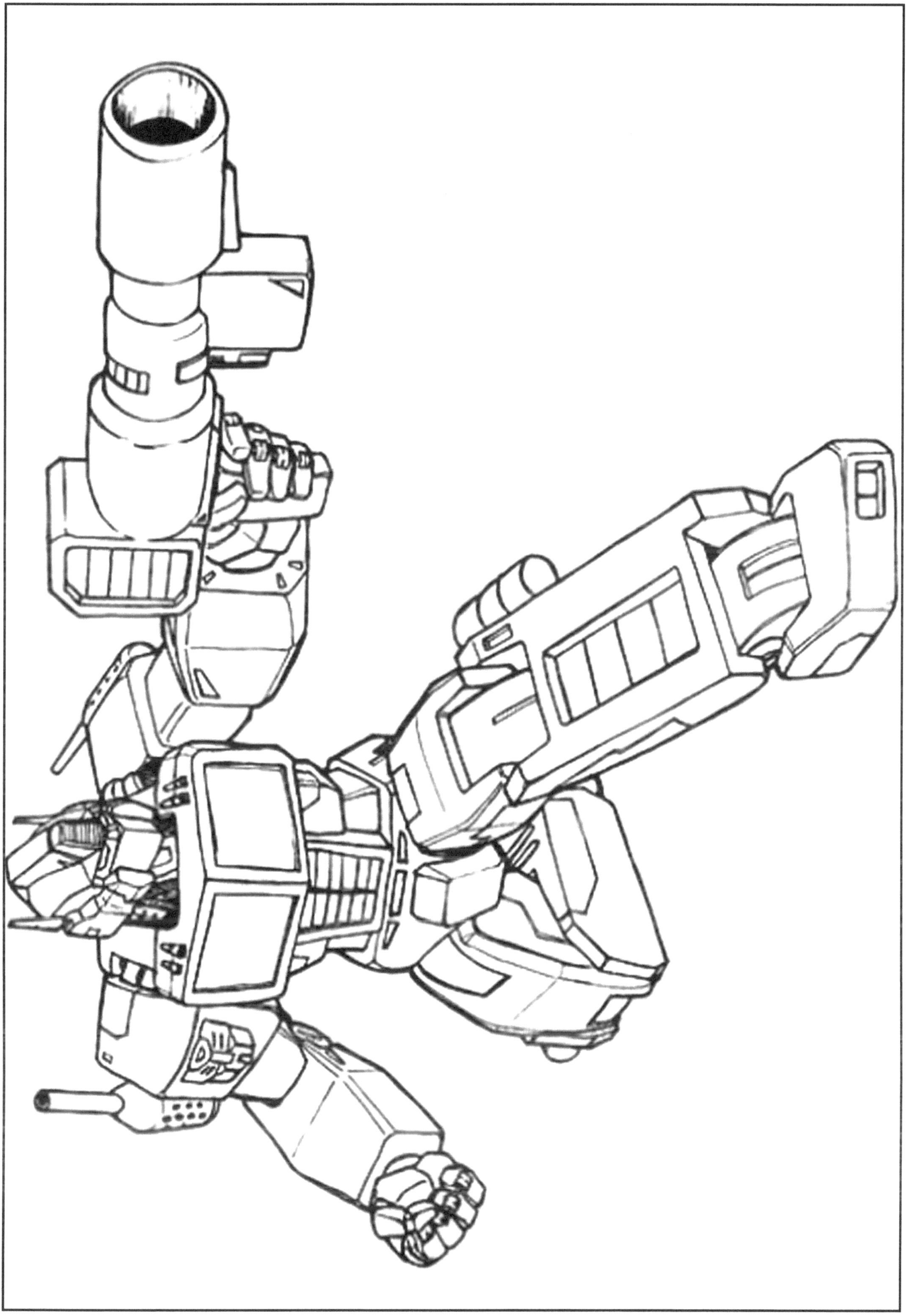

Made in United States
Troutdale, OR
07/25/2023

11560027R00064